You can lieu corn starch for flour
  And lemon milk to make it sour
  And substitute the frosting on your cake
But you must never, never, never
  Drop your standard of endeavor
  Make your lieu a work of art and not a fake

Companion book to

FIRST YOU TAKE A LEEK

IN LIEU OF...

By

MAXINE J. SALTONSTALL

With Illustrations by

WAYNE MAYFIELD

CHARLES E. TUTTLE COMPANY
Rutland, Vt. & Tokyo, Japan

Representatives
Continental Europe: BOXERBOOKS, INC.
Zurich
British Isles: PRENTICE-HALL INTERNATIONAL, INC.
London
Australasia: PAUL FLESCH & Co., PTY. LTD.
Melbourne
Canada: M. G. Hurtig Ltd.
Edmonton

*Published by the Charles E. Tuttle Company Inc.
of Rutland, Vermont & Tokyo, Japan
with editorial offices at
Suido 1-chome, 2-6, Bunkyo-ku, Tokyo, Japan*

*Production by Roland A. Mulhauser
Library of Congress Catalog Card No. 78-184811
International Standard Book Number 0-8048-1020-6*

PRINTED IN JAPAN

CONTENTS

DEDICATION

An author's dedication of his book may be done in a variety of ways. One I recall was simply "To E. K." and for all I know that may have been the neighbor's cat. Others carry on at a great rate thanking the Army, the Navy, the Marines, the Air Force, the CIA, the U.S.A. and everyone else except the one from whom they probably stole the idea in the first place.

Now I am going to take another tack—sort of down the middle of the road. There are many to whom I would wish to doff my beanie but there are a special few whom I wish to thank specifically, abundantly and without reservation. If it were possible their images would greet the morning sun from Mount Rushmore—a testimony to friendship for all to gaze upon in wonderment. Sometimes I think Virginia Carroll invented the whole idea. It was she who suggested the wildly funny title, "First you Take A Leek" from which sprang the book on leek cookery that fathered this offspring. Besides this practical event, over the years she has seen me through more tight spots than the draw string on a fat lady's corset.

In Honolulu, Opie and Margaret Cody not only deserve space on this monumental tribute but should be immortalized in poem or song. At times they have made available to me their home, their car, and thank goodness a pulpit stand dictionary, without which I could never have gone beyond the title of this book.

Herman Kragt in Beverly Hills would say with the apostle, "Silver and gold have I none but such as I have give I thee". It is marvelous to ponder the fact that his encouragement was as enthusiastically offered in the development of these few pages as it would have been had the desired result been the compilation of the Library of Congress. Ye gods!

And to the entire William Chapel family in

Los Angeles I owe more than a word of thanks. Recently I nested with them for a month on R & R*—gaining the impetus to continue on my way.

Paeans of gratitude from this peon go to my sister and her husband, Louise and Clay Huff

Borrowed from the military meaning rest and recreation

of Hermosa Beach, California whose greatness of heart is matched only by their culinary talents.

And most surely the likenesses of those two great belles of Southern California, Cynthia Ising and Frances Mercer, would more than enhance the skyline of Mount Rushmore. Each has tolled of friendship in tones as clarion as Big Ben.

Such friends are indeed the jewels in my crown.

So to you, my dear, dear friends I dedicate this book.

—THERE IS NO LIEU

FOR FRIENDSHIP—

A LIEU IS BORN

Some of the great recipes of civilized man are the result of make-do. The French call it "employez un ersatz" but then they also call stew "ragout" and turkey fritters "beignets de rechaufle de dinde" and even plain old sauerkraut and sausage becomes "choucroute garni". But you and I are not going to board this tony express—we are going to call a spade a spade and unless we are dining in Paris, poissone will be known as fish.

Fourscore and seven years before Abraham Lincoln made his remarkable address, our fathers not only brought forth upon this continent "A nation dedicated to the proposition that all men are created equal" but their stalwart wives brought forth some mighty stalwart fare. There was no running to the corner market for a frozen dinner or a kwiki-kake-mix when uninvited guests dropped in. You made-do, baby. I have no doubt that succotash, which was invented by the Indians, came about because Squaw

Evening Star's mother-in-law dropped in and there wasn't enough corn in the pot so she (Evening Star) threw in some lima beans and voila—succotash.

So make-do has often proved to be a blessing in disguise and, if it's done with a little flair you are entitled to call it a Lieu.

Here's an example—

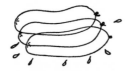

Hot Dog!

Many years ago when I lived in Hollywood, California I knew a movie director who owned a dog which he loved only a little less than his few good critical notices.

This time period was at the beginning of the mass exodus to Europe of the tax dodgers, the teetering talent that was too light for a heavy part and too heavy for a light part, the has-beens, the never-weres and the usual minutiae and camp followers. This bird was a fit in any and all categories—and he was among the first to take himself and his questionable talent—but not his dog—to Jolly Old.

Dog would have had to stay in quarantine for six months and to director's everlasting credit he did not want to subject Dog to such a ghastly confinement. So he became my howling houseguest. He was one of those great grizzly looking English bull dogs that has a dour no-nonsense appearance and a pussycat disposition. He hated exercise in any form but had an appetite like a logger's mule. All that food energy must have gone into his snore, which could rattle windows— and therein lies the plot to this tale. Or is it tail?

There were to be only six of us at dinner. I had a tiny apartment which opened on to a bougainvillaea-covered patio—making a perfect atmosphere for the few of us to enjoy the romantic feeling of an outdoor summer evening in California. It was a lovely setting.

The small oval table in the patio was covered
with a deep green linen cloth that fell to the

lawn and blended so perfectly it gave the effect in the moonlight that the table accouterments were floating in air.

The menu was exciting but simple—

Crown Rib Lamb Roast (or Pork)
Asparagus with Lemon/Butter Sauce
Whipped Potatoes
Tomatoes Vinaigrette with Watercress
Dessert   Coffee

This was my first go at a crown roast and it looked g-o-o-d! It was pretty too, with frilly, colored paper pants topping each chop to give the crown a festive air—and the stuffing all plumped up in the center like a teddy bear's belly. The market had especially good asparagus that morning and served with a simple lemon/butter sauce it made a perfect complement to the roast and light-as-air mashed potatoes. Let me here suggest, if you decide on pork instead of lamb also lieu the asparagus for broccoli and serve with the same lemon/butter sauce. Ice cold tomatoes vinaigrette with a few sprigs of watercress completed the fare—except for incidentals—but none of these are in-

volved in the story—so back to the roast.
When it was done I removed it from the
oven and proudly placed it and the round
platter it was on—on a little milking stool
that was kept in a corner of the kitchen.

A roast should always sit—or set—for a
few minutes before serving—and this count-
down period is sauce-making time, rolls out
of the oven time, salad out of the fridge
time, short prayers to the Gods of Gour-
mets time— and with all this time-time it is
most understandable how a harried hostess
would be unaware of even a good-sized dog
standing transfixed over a large display of
well padded and savory bones in the shape
of a beautiful roast—and salivating buckets
—but *buckets*—all over this vision!

The asparagus had just been gently placed
on its serving dish when I turned and saw
him. In one horrible moment I wanted to
cry, scream, faint, or simply take to my bed
and forget the whole thing. But you can't
do that, you know—stiff upper lip, the show
must go on, and in this case, if at first you
don't succeed, etc.

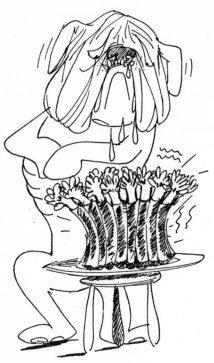

It hurts even yet to recall the total loss of that roast (for human consumption). However, don't forget Dog was a big hero in his own eyes because he had not touched the "No-No", so instead of hitting him over the head with the platter which was my immediate and natural impulse—he and all his flea bitten friends had bits and bites of roast lamb for several days. Now, the point is not that Dog's life was spared, but rather that by imaginative substitutions the evening was turned into one of the best fun dinners I have ever had.

The music was switched from violins to brass, bright lights replaced candles (proving you can lieu most anything), and I prowled for food.

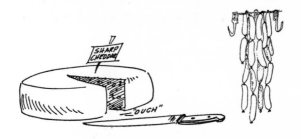

In the emergency larder were two packages of juicy, fat frankfurters, some sharp cheddar cheese, and one of those small jars of pimientos. First, the franks were placed in boiling water, covered, and let stand for about eight minutes. Meanwhile into the already whipped potatoes was added one tablespoon instant minced onion, a few parsley flakes, and the pimientos. The franks were then split open lengthwise (not completely severed), spread with mustard (I used a prepared hot type), stuffed with the jazzed-up mashed potatoes—some of that good nippy cheese was grated over the tops and under the broiler they went for about 4 minutes to brown lightly. Everything else was served as planned—howbeit a bit more on the casual than grand style.

So the evening was not only saved—it was a four star hit. A real lieu-lieu of a make-do!

Crown Roast Lamb with Lieus

If your butcher is still speaking to you after you have told him you want a crown roast, ask him if he will please crack the back bone and scrape the ends of the bones that form the crown. This insures easy carving. Allow two ribs to each fortunate guest. Leave the meat out of the fridge long enough to get it at room temperature before cooking. Insert several slivers of garlic here and there around the crown. Do not salt the meat but put Worcertershire sauce all over it. Now, dears, there are more opinions on palatable stuffing than there are on the state of the Union—so to uncomplicate the situation let's keep ours simple.

Moisten a regular standard dressing with a bit of fresh orange juice and toss in a few springs of finely chopped mint. Gently and not too firmly pack this into the cavity of the crown, cover the rib ends with individual pieces of foil or bits of raw potato to prevent their burning and cook in a pre-heated oven at 325°—allowing 30 to 35 minutes per pound—depending upon your preference for medium or well. When this thing of beauty is done and removed from the oven—as it is "setting" in a warm place (about 15 minutes), replace the foil, or whatever, with lace paper panties or, even better, kumquats. Anyone with a little imagination could really get carried away with something like this to work on.

SPRING LAMB

Let us say it is not the season for fresh, spring lamb—(only at gun point would I use frozen)—but your kindly butcher has on hand some fine pork. All the preparations remain the same as with the lamb crown except the seasoning and dressing are

PORK ROAST

lieued. If you are reading this aloud to someone you might hold his interest by having him think he is in for some "dirty dressing"! Anyway, omit the slivers of garlic and the Worcertershire and use either soya or teri-yaki sauce and shake on a goodly amount of powdered ginger. The dressing remains basically simple: in lieu of the orange juice splash in some very dry sauterne to moisten it and omit the mint. Tiny apples could embelish the crown or, if you're Liz Taylor you could use your diamonds—it's all a matter of taste.

Remember the tomatoes with sauce vinaigrette? Well, this recipe calls for olive oil so, if those of you who are beginners at marketing and cooking will allow me, may

I make a suggestion? Most olive oil containers will be marked "pure"—and although this is highly commendable in a

young lady it does not mean a diddly bop in olive oil. Here you don't fool around with

anything less than "virgin". This, obviously, means it is of the first pressing—whereas "pure" could be the second, third or even the fourth and may not have even a distant relation taste to the olive.

The Vinaigrette sauce is made by combining
1/3 cup olive oil
1 1/2 teaspoons green pepper, parsley and, if you like, capers—all finely minced
1 tablespoon onion—also finely minced
Salt and pepper
Let this stand for about an hour and then beat in *3 tablespoons cider vinegar*.

Si, We Have no Frijoles!

Puerto Vallarta is everything you have ever heard about it—good, bad and indifferent. I put in about six months there and got to know it very well indeed.

The house I called home, through the gracious hospitality of Lupe Quirk, its Mexican/

American owner, was quite a scatter. It sits majestically and grandly on a hill that overlooks everything including the Richard

Burtons. Ava Gardner rented it during the filming of "Night of the Iguana" and I guess what with the occupancy of one person or another—and perhaps mainly during the "At Home" season of Lupe and her astonishingly handsome husband, Akeley—about every notable to set foot in P.V. has passed through the iron grille doors of Casa de la Luna at one season or another.

All the terraces of the casa (I have never counted them) open on to an unmolested view of the sea and smogless sky—and it was from this place of uninhibited beauty and moonlit tranquility that a small group of us listened to the news of the first moon walk on a powerful short wave radio with the Voice of America. (No TV in P.V.).

In our patriotic zeal we had prepared a good ol' all-American fried chicken dinner—mashed potatoes and gravy, peas, biscuits, salad and fresh peach sundae. As we hung

on every word of the progress report we women unashamedly cried tears of pride and excitement as the men sat tense and silent—giving only occasional voice to their emotions as one of our boys up there was about to take the most portentious first step in history. It was an eerie and highly emotional experience and some time I would like to tell you all about it. But for now, to prove that one can even lieu the memory of a moon walk I shall give in its place the saga of a heart-rending Mexican tragedy.

You are now somewhat acquainted with the house except I would like to add it was also the constant object of tourist shutter bugs and the just plain curious. So, one day when Bob and Ruth Merrimer—a husband and wife photographer/writer team who live in P.V. and have all the equipment necessary to produce travel and airline commercials—called on me (no telephones either) and asked if they could bring in a cameraman from ABC-TV and a reporter from Oakland, California, I was not too surprised—and consented. They wanted to photograph and do a story on entertainment in the Puerto Vallarta home life of an American tourist.

Now in contrast to my home life Mary Poppins was a real swinger so my plan was to make up in hospitality and culinary prowess what might appear to be lacking in bombastic, gung-ho type whoopee.

The unanimous vote was to keep the food Mexican and simple—which resulted in a menu of barbecued spareribs, Ruth's special frijoles, garlic bread*, salad, fruit compote, coffee and incidentals. The Merrimers arrived early so Ruth could put her casuela of frijoles in the oven to cook slowly until needed. This casuela was a spectacular pot-

*Pg. 12 "First You Take A Leek."

tery dish that measured 16 inches in diameter and was a full six inches deep. Full of beans it must have weighed fifteen pounds.

As dinner time drew near we ran through a rehearsal of what we were to do when the actual shooting was to take place. Carmen, Lupe's crack cook and indispensable woman of many talents was to usher in the guests, Paulino, the mozo (houseboy) had rehearsed serving refreshments, and Maria Elena, Carmen's pretty sister, shyly fluttered around here and there pretending to do this and that. The rehearsal went very well so the scene was shot without incident —only the usual overacting and giggles natural to amateurs. Then it was decided to move into the spacious kitchen, have me take the frijoles (which were now bubbling and smelling divine) out of the oven and place them on the tile serving bar as the entire cast hovered in hand clapping admiration. Rosselini would have torn out his remaining two hairs if he could have witnessed the total confusion in the preparation of this scene. But at last the moment arrived—the special lights were properly blinding everyone, the camera was recording every well rehearsed smile, and I opened the oven door with the look of expecting to see the Hope diamond. Firmly grasping the casuela handle in my well mittened hands I swung around to face the camera which was aimed dead on me, when the sheer weight of the bean pot caused its severance from the handle and it plummeted to the floor! I was ankle deep in wall-to-wall beans. Now if I were editing that film for ABC I think I would cut most everything but that one scene because the look on our faces as that loaded casuela thundered to the floor must have been the funniest bit of the season. Only five seconds before we were all being so grand and suddenly we are up to there in hot baked beans.

Up to that time I had been especially fond of Carmen—not only because I admired her talent in the kitchen but we had also become

good friends. She would correct my lousy
Spanish with the same firmness as she ap-
plied to her seven year old son's manners
(they were perfect)—and I would correct
her lousy English with the same firmness as
I would apply to baking a souffle. Anyway,
this time she went too far—she not only

stole the scene—she stole the whole show.
While I was still standing there wondering
what to do with a useless terra cotta handle
she had literally leaped into action and was
well into the act of preparing some of her
great Mexican rice. (In case you don't rec-
ognize it, that's the lieu for the beans—but
I shall conclude the story). By the time we
all returned from hosing off our feet out by
the swimming pool, Carmen's rice was
ready to be served along with the other
dishes that had been kept hot and/or cold
respectively.

I guess it was all quite a success because
after the dinner had been filmed and the
camera and lights were gently returned to
their safe cases we all repaired to the pool
from which the sur-
rounding Mexican pop-
ulace could hear a fine
sextet harmonizing in
"Si, We Have No Fri-
joles" to the memorable
tune (to some of us) of
"Yes, We Have No
Bananas."

Carmen's Rice

There is no point in giving the recipe for Ruth's frijoles because they are only a lovely odoriferous memory—but here is Carmen's rice which is surely a wonderful lieu for spilled or any other kind of beans. The only change I will make will be in the amounts of the contents. Carmen was never known to cook for only six or eight people—even if that was the number expected at table. I think she always hoped a simile of Pancho Villa and his heroic caballeros would drop in—and believe me she was ever ready.

The amounts listed below are cut down to serve only three or four persons.

1 cup long grain rice (no washing necessary)
4 tablespoons oil
2 cups boiling water
2 cloves garlic
1 chopped onion
1 can stewed tomatoes (2-cup size)
1 can pimientos (4 oz.)
Salt, pepper, paprika

Carmen also used a casuela but you may use anything from your favorite skillet to a Pyrex dish—as long as it can be set over direct heat and covered.

LONG RICE

Let the oil get fairly hot—then slowly stir in the rice. When it becomes golden brown add the water. Toss in the rest of the ingredients—put on the cover—and that's it. Reduce the heat to simmer and after about 12 minutes check to see if more water is needed. Total cooking time should take about one-half hour—perhaps a little less. Muy sabrosa.

K. O. L. Pancakes

The Northwestern part of the United States is never referred to other than as the great Northwest. I suppose then, if one gets up into Canada it becomes the tremendous or gargantuan Northwest.

Anyway, once upon a time in the inner regions of Northern Canada there lived a kind old lady who made the "best damned pancakes I ever ate" to quote my brother-in-law. Now this K.O.L. had no fairy godmother nor did she have chickens, so it was very difficult for her to keep fresh eggs on hand. This was also before the days of pancake and waffle prepared mixes so everything was made from scratch. It would only be space consuming to here offer a full pancake recipe as that can be found any place— but let me say they all include eggs. So, one day soon after K.O.L. became a bride and went to live in the deep woods with her woodsman Lochinvar—she awakened early and fired up her wood stove to fix her man some pancakes. No eggs!! So guess what K.O.L. did kiddies? She measured out a level tablespoon of cornstarch in lieu of each needed egg and the result was wonderful.

After this she even lieued corn starch for eggs in her cakes—and everyone lived happily ever after.

As a postscript you should know that I have never tested this but my brother-in-law is so honest that he only tells tall fish tales.

The author is aware of the fact that in certain instances in these pages the word "lieu" is not used in its strictest sense. For example: in selecting a crown roast of pork in place of lamb cooked in the same beautiful manner, is really not a "lieu". But to use 1 level tablespoon of corn starch in lieu of each egg required in a recipe *is* lieu in its strictest sense.

Last fall semester, while still living in Honolulu, I sought and was given many helpful suggestions on food substitutions from the Home Economics Department of the University of Hawaii. Some of the following are among the most commonly used—while other suggestions will be made along the way.

1 cup sifted flour: 7/8 cup sifted hard wheat all purpose flour minus 2 tablespoons.
1 cup all purpose flour: 1⅛ cups (1 cup plus 2 tablespoons) pastry flour.
1 tablespoon flour for thickening: ½ table-

spoons corn starch, potato starch, rice starch, or arrowroot starch or $\frac{2}{3}$ table-spoon quick cooking tapioca.

1 cup honey: 1$\frac{1}{4}$ cups sugar plus $\frac{1}{4}$ cup liquid, or equal amount light molasses.

1 ounce chocolate: 3 tablespoons cocoa plus 1 tablespoon fat.

1 cup butter: 1 cup margarine; or 7/8 to 1 cup hydrogenated fat plus 1 tablespoon fat; or 7/8 cup lard plus $\frac{1}{2}$ teaspoon salt; or 7/8 cup rendered fat plus $\frac{1}{2}$ teaspoon fat.

1 cup corn syrup: 1 cup sugar plus $\frac{1}{4}$ cup liquid.

1 cup coffee cream (20%): 3 tablespoons butter plus about 7/8 cup milk.

1 cup whole milk: 1 cup reconstituted non-fat dry milk plus 2$\frac{1}{2}$ teaspoons butter or margarine; or $\frac{1}{2}$ cup water plus $\frac{1}{2}$ cup canned evaporated milk.

1 cup milk: 3 tablespoons sifted non-fat dry milk powder plus 1 cup water, or 6 table-spoons sifted non-fat dry milk crystals plus 1 cup water.

1 cup buttermilk or sour milk: 1 tablespoon vinegar or lemon juice plus enough sweet milk to make 1 cup (let it stand five minutes); or 1$\frac{3}{4}$ teaspoons cream of tartar plus 1 cup sweet milk; or an equal amount of yogurt.

1 teaspoon baking powder: ¼ teaspoon baking soda plus ½ cup fully-soured milk or buttermilk; or ¼ teaspoon baking soda plus 5/8 teaspoon cream of tartar. If the recipe calls for molasses use ¼ teaspoon baking soda plus ½ cup light molasses. If blackstrap molasses is called for use only ¼ cup. Another combination is ¼ teaspoon baking soda plus ½ tablespoon vinegar or lemon juice used with sweet milk to make ½ cup.

1 whole egg: 2 egg yolks; or 3 tablespoons thawed frozen eggs; or 2½ tablespoons dry whole egg powder plus 2½ tablespoons lukewarm water.

1 egg yolk: 1½ tablespoons frozen egg yolk; or 2 tablespoons sifted dry egg yolk powder plus 2 tablespoons water.

1 egg white: 2 tablespoons frozen egg white; or 2 teaspoons sifted dry egg white powder plus 2 tablespoons water.

1 cup seedless raisins: 1 cup chopped dried prunes.

1 cup sugar: 1¾ cups packed-down confectioners' sugar. In baking, 1 cup molasses plus ¼ to ½ teaspoon baking soda—but omit the baking soda called for in the recipe.

1 tablespoon vinegar: 1 tablespoon of dry wine or lemon juice.

Now, for you readers who are advanced enough in the knowledge of cookery to know the difference between an umlaut and an omelet—let's have some fun with spices and herbs. Next time a recipe calls for *basil* —answer with *oregano,* or, contrarywise lieu *oregano* with *basil* or *marjorum.* If you are out of *allspice*—for the equivalent of 1 teaspoon, lieu ½ teaspoon *cinnamon* plus ⅛ teaspoon *cloves.* In place of *mace—nutmeg;* or vice versa. No ready-mix *pumpkin pie spice?* Blend ½ teaspoon *cinnamon,* ¼ teaspoon *ginger,* ⅛ teaspoon *nutmeg* and ⅛ teaspoon *cloves.* Try *sage* in place of *rosemary* —*saffron* for *turmeric* or *tumeric* for *saffron.*

Bouillabaisse a Deux

There will be no anecdote or story with which to preface this beautiful bouillabaisse recipe. I figure if you make it properly it is so good you are liable to conjure up a present situation of your own making that would prove to be more interesting than any vicarious experience.

Contrary to what you may think if you have never made bouillabaisse and have seen it only on the menu at your favorite dining out place—be assured it is no more difficult to accomplish than a half gainer off a low board! I'm only half kidding—but go about it this way—(the bouillabaisse—not the half gainer). See to it that you have an enameled, teflon or stainless steel pan. This being a recipe for only 2 persons I would suggest a 2 quart size. This will give the fish plenty of room to sozzle around in the juice.

The fish may consist of clams, mussells, lobster tails, fillet of flounder, oysters, crab meat, red snapper, cod, haddock, scallops, sea bass, and for all you guys—float a mermaid if you can find one. If clams and/or

mussels are used be sure and scrub them mightily. Any two or more of these or any other fish you have on hand will work out fine. Bouillabaisse means "A mess of fish" and it would be almost impossible to go wrong on any combination you may choose.

Cut the cuttable pieces in about 1 to 2 inches in size. Now, take a leek, and the onion and garlic, and dice them together with a good sized tomato. Saute this for 5 minutes in

butter—about the size of a walnut—my mother used to say. For the liquid you may use a brimming cup of clam juice and ½ cup of water—or a combination of an 8-oz. can of tomato sauce mixed with ½ cup of dry white wine—or even a chicken bouillon cube dissolved in a cup of hot water. Also, if oysters are added by all means use their liquor. Anyway, whatever liquid your fancy dictates, add to the sauteed fish, etc. and before it starts simmering let yourself go and add any or all of the following: dash of saffron, touch of cayenne, shake of paprika, bit of pepper (preferably white), seasoned salt to taste, and a few drops of Worcestershire or Tabasco sauce. Cover the pan and

let it simmer until the shell fish open (about 15 minutes). Do not overcook this succulent dish. If you are fortunate enough to own two small earthenware casseroles—serve the bouillabaisse individually in these and top each with a slice of French garlic bread. (*First You Take A Leek—p. 12*).

Some dark and stormy night when you had thought about making a big pot of clam chowder—lieu—do this instead and maybe

your husband will get into such a good mood he will let you go to that big dress sale the next day!

Sauerkraut Salad

(WOULD YOU BELIEVE IT?)

Making the following recipe known to the public is tantamount to exposing the plans of Sandy Hook in war time.

Very seldom do I keep a recipe secret but with this one I've had so much fun making guests try to guess the ingredients that I kind of hate to give it away and spoil the fun. On the other hand half the pleasure of enjoying anything is in the sharing—so when you make this delectable dish take a sample to your neighbor and she may forgive you for playing the TV too loud last night.

Remember in *First You Take a Leek* how I mentioned my fondness for cabbage in any form? Well this is a continuation of that thought. Here you have an ice cold sauerkraut salad that you must make to believe. This recipe makes one and a half quarts and

be assured you will have no trouble getting
rid of it.*

Mix together:
1 *large can sauerkraut—#2 1/2 size or two*
   #303 cans
1 *medium onion diced*
1 *medium green pepper diced*
1 *cup celery sliced thin*
1 1/4 *cups sugar*
1/2 *cup oil*
1/2 *cup vinegar*
Let stand 24 hours
Next time you're thinking of having cole
slaw—lieu this instead. Although it's the
perfect complement to ham or pork, I have
served it very successfully with casual ham-
burgers, hot dogs, casserole dishes, barbe-
cues, etc.

*How *not to get rid of it follows:*

How NOT to
Get Rid of It

Last year for a few weeks in Honolulu I had a room-mate named Helen Westfall. We had a great system worked out for kitchen duties. To Helen KP was strictly therapeutic and on the other hand to me cooking is a form of art. True, some artists are of the Rube Goldberg school, a few are in the Rembrandt class, but I just go along like Grandma Moses doin' my own thing. Anyway—neither Helen nor I would ever bother the other one while each was at her own task except—one day. I had prepared a large jar of this sauerkraut salad and had placed it on the top shelf of the refrigerator to marinate and to get good and cold as a surprise for dinner the following evening. Helen decided to clean the fridge. I was in the living room working the Sunday crossword puzzle and as I looked up to ask Helen for a five letter word for an East Indian tree (she's smarter than I) I saw that she had opened the sauerkraut jar and was about to up-end it into the disposal. You should have heard me bellow! How one can bellow and broad jump at the same time I don't know but I made that kitchen in one grand leap.

At the first bel Helen froze and thinking she was at the very least holding a hot bottle of carbontetrochloride she remained immobile for at least thirty seconds after I pried the jar out of her hands. Poor Helen— she discovered how emotional I can get— even over sauerkraut. When she surfaced she explained she hadn't noticed the jar before (reminds me of the old vaudeville joke with the tag line "What elephant?") and when she opened it and smelled the contents she thought that whatever it was had been dead a long, long time and she'd better get rid of it. But that's sauerkraut kids—the first whiff may rock you back on your heels —but stay in there 'cause when the fog clears you're going to like it. Helen did.

Weight Here

Everyone is either on a diet or wishes he were. Actually, when I diet everybody in my house is happy—including myself—because I am inclined to give more thought to the seasoning and preparation of, let's say a cheese omelet, knowing it will be the big meal of the day—than would be given to a lasagne casserole with its accompaniment of garlic bread, salad, etc. etc. ad calorieitum.

I am not prescribing a diet. That must be done professionally. However, almost all diets for simple loss of weight will contain the foods I hope to make more interesting for you.

As an example—instead of the usual sliced cold tomato, why not bake it whole? Put a couple of tablespoons of water in a pan, slice a tiny piece from the bottom of the tomato so it will not roll over, scoop out a little hole in the top and dampen the skin

just enough to hold some seasoned salt and basil, which should be sprinkled generously all over—plus into the little hole in the top. Bake about eight minutes in a medium hot oven. It really needs only to warm through. This would be delicious with a piece of filet of sole* which has been poached in onion bouillon** (onion bouillon cubes are available in most markets) to which has been added a bay leaf and a few tablespoons of very dry sauterne. Easy on the salt—the bouillon cube may be salty enough. To add both beauty and nourishment with few extra calories to your dinner plate cook up some frozen broccoli accented with lemon or lime juice. If more than one is on a diet—expand recipe accordingly.

Halibut, sea bass, or even shrimp.
**In most good fish markets you will find spices especially prepared for poaching. In case you go this route (which is highly recommended), a little onion, garlic and/or celery may be added. The bouillon idea is suggested only as a quick easy method. Also refer to the "Pot-Pourri" chapter and find more ideas on fish stock.*

Seviche!

The drive from Mexico City to Acapulco is truly spectacular. After leaving the city one passes through such picturesque villages as Tres Marias (better known as Tres Tequilas), Cuernavaca, Taxco, Chilpancingo, and Zihuatanejo—but for all I saw on my first trip we could have been on the Old Oregon Trail—because we were traveling by night. The reason for this nocturnal exodus was quite logical and simple. It had taken us all day to say goodbye to everyone, get all of our gear loaded and get on the road. There were three of us—my daughter who was about $3\frac{1}{2}$ then, and a young American friend of my nephew's who proved to be an excellent driver, and I. Since that time I would say I have driven back and forth over that same road more times than can be recalled—but from the first clear daylight view of the ground covered that night—my nightmares started. There are

only about two dares I would not take for even a thousand dollars—one is to drive the Mexico City-Acapulco road at night, and the other is to eat poi. I love Mexico and Mexicans and frijoles and everything else south of the border—and I think Hawaii and Hawaiians and papayas and mangoes and all that stuff are simply swell—but nobody can convince me that Mexican roads are safe at night or that poi is tasty. But on to the dawn arrival in Acapulco.

Anyone who has ever made this trip at any time of day or night can tell you as you reach the mountain top just before the outskirts of the city, very abruptly the entire panorama of Acapulco Bay comes into view.

Wham! Just like that—there it is. You have to be awe struck by such incredible beauty. It might be interesting to consider the thoughts this startling scene conjured up in each of us at that moment. My daughter, who by this time had had a full night's sleep and was more than wide awake, no doubt figured Walt Disney was responsible for the whole thing so it had to be good. My nephew's young friend, I'm sure, pictured nothing but girls, girls, girls. I not only imagined but craved nothing more than a quiet spot under a softly swaying palm tree because after recovering from coming face to face with such vivid lovliness the only thing I could think of was sleep, sleep, sleep. Hours and hours and days and days. But not in Mexico, baby. Forget all that business about the cock crowing at dawn

and the early morning song of the Meadow
Lark. Bah! Humbug! In Mexico the cock
crows all night long and the cacophony of
bird voices from sun down to sun up is
matched only by the constant idiocy of
barking dogs and the maddening din of
hundreds of juke boxes—all of which have
one volume—wide open. So, after our brief
and bleary-eyed pause at the gateway to this
Eden that is Acapulco, we found our hotel

where friends made us welcome even at that jarring hour. By ten o'clock we were all

gathered on the *morning beach*—prompt and as bent on throwing ourselves into the sea as the lemmings. I was initiated into the daily ritual of following this first swim with a dish of ice cold seviche. Seviche! The very word makes my taste buds leap into play.

Good seviche is so hot that after one bite you can crack a glass if you exhale on it. What chicken soup is to the Jew, seviche is to the Mexican. It is considered better than oxygen for what ails you—even as chicken soup is affectionately known as Jewish penicillin. It is my considered opinion that great

plagues could be annihilated if all peoples subsisted solely on these two powerful dishes. Matter of fact, I think I would rise up from the black plague itself if offered either one. Oh, to be a Mexican-Jew! Un-

fortunately, seviche cannot be prepared outside of Mexico with the same hair-raising results one gets with all the original ingredients called for—because nowhere else can be found the fresh chiles verdes (hot green chiles), or celandro (a musky herb indigenous to Mexico and used as we use parsley). However, I shall give you two recipes—the Mexican and an excellent lieu—and you may play it piquante or mild to your own liking.

In Mexico, a fish called "sierra" is most often used, although bonito or any other white fish is just as tasty. Using the filet, it is cut into pieces between bite and chopped size. This is marinated in lime juice for about an hour—keeping it very cold. Then

are added finely chopped chiles, chopped fresh tomatoes, a touch of celandro and a little minced garlic and onion. It is chilled for at least another half hour and then it is ready to shoot off sparks. It's just like eating ground glass—and I love it!

State-side style can be just as "piquante"— only the flavor will differ slightly because of a few lieus. Still using any white, non-fatty fish start your preparation in the same manner as above. Now, use a combination of lemon and lime juice for the marinade. Mexican limes are a little different (and far superior) in flavor than ours—making them more versatile and widely used. It is a common practice below the border to use a few drops of lime juice over soft boiled eggs, soups, etc. It is great for bringing up the flavor. But to return—after the fish has "cooked" for the required hour, the chiles are lieued with a dash or two of Tabasco sauce. This should jolt the old gastric juices into action—if it doesn't stop your heart first! Add the chopped tomatoes, garlic and onion—and again lieu—this time parsley for celandro. Let it chill again as the flavors blend and serve it as you would any other seafood cocktail meant for dragons.

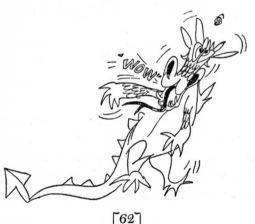

Breakfast Anyone?

This is such a good lieu for the standard brands of dry breakfast cereals that you may come to prefer the substitute and reverse the lieu.

Some morning when your taste buds are more speculative than anticipatory, take some of that Ry-Krisp you have left over from your diet daze and crumble it with the rolling pin, crisp it in the oven for a few moments, add your favorite fruit, milk, and sugar—and there you have it—Ambrosia. No Ry-Krisp? Use ordinary bread crumbs. Rye, wheat, white, anything—you'll love it.

Oh to Have a Crêpe in Paris

NOW THAT SPRING IS HERE

In Paris, across the street from "The Drug Store" and down a few blocks, off the Champ Elyseés, is a little place that specializes in crêpes. They do not use a crêpe pan as you would in your own home, but have special gas-heated round grills which are in the center of the little restaurant so the customers may watch in awe, curiosity, boredom or whatever as the chef pours, fills and folds these delicacies.

This jewel of a place was recommended to my daughter and me by the concierge of our hotel—for which he became the recipient of many American goodies from the Paris P.X.

The menu was endless—and when we moved from our hotel on the Rue de Berri—which was only a few blocks away—to an apartment on the Left Bank,* which was clear

*First I must tell you why we moved.

[64]

across town, we had to discontinue our ad-
ventures in completing their list of sugges-

tions. Instead, our gluttony took on another form and we concentrated on the bakery directly across the street where they put forth fresh bread and rolls twice a day. Lordy! The memory of it is still enough to make me quiver—I can smell it now. So, before I am tempted to digress and give you

a recipe for Croissante or French bread— we shall get on with the crêpes.

Don't let the idea of making crêpes scare you. Just as bouillabaisse is only fish soup— crêpes are simply glorified pancakes. To be sure, it will serve you well to "think

French" as you proceed because even a spinach and raw egg crêpe calls for a bit of savoir faire in the serving.

The typically Parisienne and charming hotel room we first occupied had one drawback. In the bathroom was a bathtub, a wash basin

and a bidet—but the loo* was down the hall! This bit of French reasoning proved to be most disconcerting to my direct Yankee way of thinking—and although in the States I had enjoyed many a progressive dinner

*This is not the masculine gender of lieu— it has a hole different meaning.

party (you know, shrimp coctails at good ol' Joe's—soup and salad at Herb's and Mary's—barbecue at the Martin's new place) I could see no reason to carry this program over into my habits of nature. It completely boggled me—and to put a stop to my speeches on the subject and to stay my hand from writing a letter to the editor of the Paris Tribune—my daughter suggested we move. So we moved—and even though the new apartment was six flights up with no elevator—it was fully equipped.

It is all but imperative to have a real French-type crêpe pan. Justify the small

expense by considering it an excellent investment because of the money saved by this glamorous way of utilizing your leftovers. And contrarywise, what better way to dramatize the finale of an exquisite meal. Flambé-ant, I call it.

Let me stress here—and please make this an unbreakable rule in your kitchen—that the crêpe pan must never—not even once—be used for cooking any other foods. Before its

debut see that it is thoroughly scrubbed—
then more than half filled with oil and put
over a low heat. The oil need not get hot -

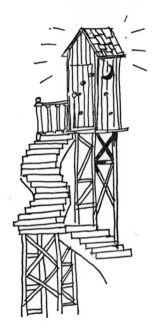

hot—just warm - hot—and let this stand in
the pan all night or day. No use wasting all
that good clean cooking oil—so pour it into
a jar or back into the bottle and use it for
french frying onions or something. Wipe
out the excess oil with a paper towel and
now you have a beautiful crêpe pan ready

for action. Each time before the pan is used put in about 1 tablespoon of oil—see that it covers the surface, let it get hot and then discard it. Now, with a large spoon put enough batter into the pan to completely cover the bottom, rolling the pan to expedite the spreading. If too much batter gets into the pan (crêpes are very thin) simply tip the excess out. (Once you have done all this you will wonder why you ever thought it might be beyond you. Matter of fact, in the time it has taken to write this you could be on your second or third batch.) At this point watch the edges of the crêpe because as soon as it starts to get golden—flip it. The flip side will go faster—so when it appears done —slide it directly from the pan into the disposal! No, it is not I who has flipped. The first crêpe is used as an oil sponge and will not be very good. So, you have had your dress rehearsal and from now on it's all your show. No more oil is needed in the pan—all signals are go———

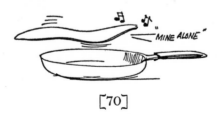

Crêpe Batter to "Go" On

3/4 cup all-purpose flour
1 egg yolk
1 whole egg
1 1/4 cups milk
Pinch of salt
1 tablespoon butter, margarine, or oil
Add the salt to the flour and sift into a bowl.
Stir in the egg yolk and one-half the milk.
Get it good and smooth and then add the
remaining milk and butter, oil or margarine.
You may use a blender, a wire whip or anything as long as the batter is very smooth—
like good coffee cream.

Following are two basic ideas for crêpes—
one a main luncheon or dinner dish—the
other a dessert. These are to serve as an
indication of the vast versatility of the crêpe
as a great lieu for the usual run-of-the-mill
type of entree or sweet. This recipe will
make approximately twelve crêpes.

Crêpes with Ham, Asparagus & Hollandaise

Make up the twelve crêpes and lay them aside. Turn the oven on to 400°. Heat two of those little cans of hollandaise sauce that can be found in most any market. I don't recommend the packaged brands but the canned is great. Planning on either three crêpes for four—or four for three—get twelve slices of thin boiled ham. About one pound of asparagus should yield enough for

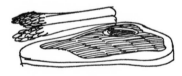

two or three spears in each crêpe. This will be washed, trimmed and boiled in salted water until tender—about 15 minutes. Now, after placing a slice of ham and the asparagus on each crêpe, roll them all up gently, place them in a buttered Pyrex or other oven-proof dish, dot with butter and bake for 12 to 15 minutes. Remove them from the oven, pour over the hollandaise sauce and serve them forth with pride and joy.

Crêpes with Blueberries

To end a meal, a day or a book—what better way than a sweet crêpe? Most dessert crêpes call for a variety of booze but, in my opinion, this only complicates matters and causes undue expense. Besides, why not have a dessert that even the kids can enjoy? In this recipe we use only ½ cup of red wine and the cooking removes the alcohol.

Figuring on twelve crêpes—get:

2 boxes blueberries
1/2 cup orange juice
4 tablespoons currant jelly
1 tablespoon arrowroot
1/2 cup red wine
Sifted confectioners sugar
Butter
Whipped or sour cream

Have ready a buttered baking dish that will hold twelve rolled or folded crêpes. Preheat oven to 400°.

After the blueberries are washed put them to one side in a Pyrex dish or similar bowl. In a saucepan combine juice and wine and bring it to the boiling point over a low heat. Dissolve the Arrowroot in 2 Tablespoons of cold water and add this gradually to the saucepan—stirring constantly. Combine it immediately with the blueberries. Put 2 or 3 Tablespoons of the mixture on each crêpe and either roll or fold them. Place them gently in the baking dish and dot each one with butter. In 15 minutes take them out and sugar them well. Top with sour or whipped cream.

I've never had a purple crêpe
I never hope to have one
But I can tell you any how
I'd rather have than be one
Apologies to
GELETT BURGESS

POT-POURRI

Put a bay leaf in flour or corn starch that has been opened—to discourage insects. Even if such things are stored in jars this is still a good idea to prevent spoilage—particularly in humid climates. The bay leaf emits no flavor.

Eggs that are being hard boiled should be moved about occasionally to keep the yolks centered.

After much experimenting with stews (no matter how that's interpreted it's true) I have found that carrots tend to sweeten the liquid. I cook mine separately and add them at the last moment before serving.

In the chapter "Weight Here", Paragraph 3, the recipe suggests poaching fish in onion bouillon. Here let me give you a basic recipe for fish stock which is ideal if you have the time to make it. For two cups of stock start with about three cups of water and add any fish parts you have or go buy some— heads, tails (sounds like a fishy coin game) bones, etc., and/or at least two cups of lean fish—Flounder, Sole, Halibut and the like. Add a small onion, quartered or chopped, 1 small carrot, a small celery stalk (leaves and all), 1/2 bay leaf and a shake or two of seasoned salt. The water should just cover the fish, so if it's necessary, start with a little more water and don't be afraid 'cause it will simmer down to two cups. In an uncovered pan this should take approximately 1/2 hour.

Now strain and taste for seasoning and you're ready to go. Don't want to go through all that? Use clam juice. It's a perfect lieu.

If the mouth of your olive oil container is large enough through which to drop a cube of sugar—do so. It will never disolve and will keep the oil from turning rancid. Do not—I repeat—do not use loose sugar. Ugh!

Add one grated raw potato to hot mashed potatoes for an absolutely divine nutty flavor.

A LIEU OF SORTS

With herbs, spices and/or condiments do not hesitate to substitute the frozen for the fresh-or the fresh for the frozen or dried. All that is necessary is to know how much of one will emit what of another in flavor. For example:

Chives. 1 tablespoon chopped fresh = 1 tablespoon freeze dried or frozen.

Garlic. 1 clove = 1/8 teaspoon garlic powder or 1/2 teaspoon garlic salt.

Onion. 1/3 cup chopped fresh = 1 tablespoon instant minced. 1/4 cup chopped fresh = 1 tablespoon dried onion flakes or 1 tablespoon onion salt.

Parsley. 3 tablespoons fresh chopped = 1 tablespoon dried parsley flakes.

Sweet Pepper. 2 tablespoons chopped fresh (green on red) = 1 tablespoon sweet pepper flakes.

Lives there a woman who does not love to clip bits from newspapers and magazines? Well, girls, I am one of you—and herewith is a copy of one of my better efforts of a long time ago. This will enable you to hang-in three with any of your overbearing alleged gourmet acquaintances.

HOW DO HERBS, SPICES AND CONDIMENTS DIFFER?

Herbs are prepared from the leafy or soft portion of certain plants, while spices are derived from roots, bulbs, flowers, fruits, barks, and seeds. Condiments are made up of combinations of spices and other ingredients. Catsup, chili sauces, prepared mustard and steak sauces are examples of common condiments. All of these products are used to enhance or accent natural food flavors or to impart a special taste.